GRAVE PARK POESY

Poems by Joseph Matose

First published in Great Britain in 2022 by:

Carnelian Heart Publishing Ltd

Suite A

82 James Carter Road

Mildenhall

Suffolk

IP28 7DE

UK

www.carnelianheartpublishing.co.uk

©Joseph Matose 2022

Paperback ISBN: 978-1-914287-23-7

Ebook ISBN: 978-1-914287-24-4

A CIP catalogue record for this book is available from the British Library.

Editors:

Dzikamayi Chando & Samantha Rumbidzai Vazhure

Cover design:

Artwork - Ganime Donmez

Layout - Rebecca Covers

Book Interior:

Typeset by Carnelian Heart Publishing Ltd

Layout and formatting by DanTs Media

Table of Contents

To my wife Portia, daughter Bridget and the four Shangane Boys!

Acknowledgements

This poetry compilation was made possible through the support and guidance rendered by school teachers. Notable is Nkosana Hleruka who taught at Chibwedziva, now Tsakani High School in 1985 during university semester holidays. His influence and guidance to me in the sphere of creative writing had a domino effect.

For his admiration of Dambudzo Marechera (who invariably became my own role model) and his personal interest in reading African Writers Series before the Class, Nkosana awakened in me a dormant desire to read and to write. For his effort he's worthy of mention.

I wouldn't have been an ardent bookworm had I not lived with Joshua Chauke (a cousin brother) in 1990. Joshua, then Principal of Malipati High School with a Master Degree in Literature from Idaho University, converted his bookroom into a sleeping quarter where he accommodated me. I had unhindered time of book-reading. In that regard, Joshua's support is highly acknowledged.

I also acknowledge the interaction I had with Nhamo; Dambudzo Marechera's sibling from whom I borrowed lots of classics that his deceased brother brought from outside the country. The 1995 year-long friendship was a turning point. It honed my perspectives and lent me an impetus to this day.

To those who continue to endure the fastidious character of a writer that is pervasive to all artists and to others who provided support (moral or material) and friends who lived with me especially while in South Africa (where with pain the Muse wrung poetry from my heart) I deeply acknowledge.

Family also, above all my wife Portia, for her endurance. Endurance of loneliness while my spirit floated and fleeted in the world of creativity. Today I salute her while pronouncing this belated acknowledgement!

Not least but last, the Editors, Samantha Rumbidzai Vazhure and Dzikamayi Chando, for their time and dedication to lathe the manuscript until its form assumed the lean shape it has achieved are sincerely acknowledged.

In particular, Samantha! May her spirit to promote fellow writers in Zimbabwe continue to shine!

Tinotenda. Hikhesile. Siyabonga.

THANK YOU.

J.M.

25 March 2022

Seen It All

Boom! Drum beat; alto, soprano and bass
Accompanied by the violent shake of bum;

In dishabille—
Naked crotches; hairy nest
Red like sour fruit pressed.

A forest of russet mushroom with two legs
Rowdy, acerbic and mad like banal *mycota*...
(I fancy I will not eat mushroom this year!)

Round and round, to the mad boom of drum
They danced their malice out till the Devil
In crotched loin cloth lifted his hand to give a toast!

Then a solid mass into a fluid of eerie acid
Poured to raze the premises under siege
And, son of man to nail on the hungry cross.

For, the Devil claims right to joint ownership
Of the world; animal, grass, tree and man
Whereby, goodness is viciously hunted down.

Macabre ensemble, waving the red finger
Pointed the way to the nearest graveyard
Diggers, instantly hired to work the rugged soil

A loan was drawn from banks to pay fat bills:
The undertaker his and mortuary its fees.
So that, the beleaguered are sure victims!

Mushroom that sprouted so red early dawn

Wilted and receded from wherever it came
Leaving a sickly stench and a sprawling rot.

The last drum boomed and like a stone fell
Into silence. The Devil then audited his books
And nodded, satisfied of the damage done.

He licked gnarled paws, folded the bushy tail
And polished the over used horns, then retired
To pensive plan of another mundane assault;

They put on the forgotten rugs
To feed the famished bugs.

Balls

In courtship decrying lucre
Sucked within rolling drums
Violent lips of balls are kissing.
The sweet din of heavy balls
Swinging, crushing, pulverizing
Releasing treasure in between.

When the teasing switch is up
Angry balls rattle up and down.
A constant gush of cold sweat—
Streak across the dry dough;
Where expectant midwives wait
Patiently, loyally and always—
For yet another golden birth!

Ode to the indefatigable Gold Ball Mills; Dalny Mine, Chakari; 11 Feb' 2013.

Books

Let us the world with books build
And minds with letters also guild.
For, those who fill heads with letters
Snap open their progeny's fetters.

I lived and also died still a learner
All was mine, I was a full earner.
Those who to toil of study disdain
Have in death some endless pain.

What have they the world to show
Nor prove they've all there's to know
To die in ignorance's domain
Gives thee less energy to rise again!

The Lust Respects

Guns of his so brazen they blazed
Thus his name they said he was Smoky
For many a victim his bullets grazed
Now lies he in this oblong choky!

The law he robbed, and bank he paid not
Resist his order at your own cost
So fast he killed, so quick he shot,
His aim made sure no bullet was lost!

They contrived that deep he be buried
His ghost to never rise again,
His memorial day too was so hurried
Fast to forget his face's close up!

Chalk for bones, white the shroud
Prostrate now forever he lies
Where no man rich or poor is proud
From the sorry day that he dies!

Her Dust Respects

So well she loved her nude
Who now is in heavy shroud
For the lust for a loose dude
Tossed her up the macabre cloud!

My sister will I not mourn
Her beauty rusted in dust!
My sister will I not mourn
Now bones her curved bust!

Time is a cruel fool I say—
It defies all that is good:
To him in pain see its odd delay
Yet quick to her in a jovial mood!

For years she'll be missed
By all, not by a forgetful few
For, whoever death has kissed
Forever she will be gone!

Acre of Death

All folks bereft of lifetime's breath
I'm now left with a family distraught
Would I not call it a place replete with nought
This sanctified acre of utter death?

Call it with all names you desire
Orphan I will call it with just one
For, when atop my sire lies a stone
Has he not gone with the heart's fire!

So, leave me with my sorrow to pine
And tears of an orphan let me weep
For, between the dead man's deep
And my cold perch is a solid line.

Have I therefore, good words for it?
Death is death and I'm overly lost,
With none to properly weigh the cost
Of losing a loved one to grit?

Writer's Autobiography

My Ma's back curved like a Rainbow
While in her womb I reclined
Then, the first sweet sound
I cried at birth: *a Manuscript*!

Born to write; I died in script.
Pregnant with poesy
I died in words—

Mark where I lie with this:
To he who succumbed
Writing chuff
Yet, nearly killed his pregnant Ma
With lingering lyrics!

Norm

Live it, eat it, dream it—
The new normal
Is to accept the old abnormal!

Pensioner's Despair

A retrenched I met who was so morose,
For whose solace this I did compose:
The golden Sun that once rose
At doom of dusk, will always close
He who ruptured from the womb
Is inevitably sealed in the tomb
For, what is left if a job you find
With despair is to leave it behind!

Previously published in TSOTSO Magazine, 19 Jan' 1997, Chegutu.

Keys

Keys of recondite design;
Skewed or shape divine
Keys of imagined length
As well as tested strength

Obliging into a hole
With equanimity of a dole
For humankind's access
And unhindered egress.

Round, flat, short or long
Light, heavy and strong
For Jail, School or Churches;
No-one unlawfully lurches.

*

Long shaft or short shaft
Thin shaft of another craft;

Blade shape, blunt shape;
Shaped as tooth o' an ape!

Only 'thing' going in 'one hole'
Willingly, be it big or small!

Keys, Keys, Keys!

To Brave Men

You, who can *only* meet defeat,
Where enemies just look at you
Whose downfall is *only* realized
When traitors care to consult you
Who can suffer loss or death
Only when detractors say *nothing!*
You are the Brave of *ALL* Men
Who *SHOULD* lead

and liberate humankind!

Conceived, 06 June 2013, Kadoma Municipal Offices.

Fiery Old Fellow

He must be old and quite angry,
The Fellow who beats drums;
Whose fire is curved and forked
And fond of torching things.

His temper is surely red hot.
With drums made of angry tin
How loud he beats and bangs,
Venting ire with a flood of tears.

He shifts position of his drums
Or, it is his wife replying him;
Here a bang, there a blast
Spitting forks of deadly fire.

Was this guy somehow wronged
Or, up the sky, banished
Yearly waiting for Summer time
To wend and vent his anger?

Lo! There is too much blaze
The entire dome is on angry fire.
Are we predecessors or are we
Progeny of his bygone arch-rivals?

His gusto is at its highest peak
You can tell by the tempest
Blown from the russet lungs
That split trees into matchsticks.
His fury knows no boundary
Churning Land and the briny deep
Tossing both boat and building

With flood of the acerbic urine!

How he executes the assault;
First, he conceals his presence
In dark, shifting sheets of cloud
Then he empties his arsenal with tireless salvo.

The rowdy aerial battlefield
Becomes quite ablaze indeed.
As he musters man and battleship
In a relentless and daring attack.

You Deserve Me

You are a man of chaste
  With love and wisdom good;
I challenge you in haste
  Do well and love me good.

You are a man for Ruth
  Whose heart is ever humble;
You are a man of truth
  One who will never stumble.

Your voice has love and wit
  You never growl or shout
In dearth you never quit
  Or in sickness have I doubt.

By compassion you rule:
  Supremacy with no flaws
Whenever you ridicule
  It is within marital laws.

You guide the boys so well,
  Modesty girls also learn;
Where both down fell
  To correct, respect to earn.

For morsels you pray;
  Thanking for all well-fed
Again, appreciate the day
  With prayer afore the bed.

A woman's praise to a good Husband. 2120 hours, 28 June 2013, Chakari.

They Pulled Him Dead

Wriggling through cracks
And corners so crooked
Stepping on sharp rocks
And loose bog that slips
They then disappear
    In the dark orifice.

With a streak on the head
Gloom they pierce or attack.
Feeling walls with wet hands
To fumble for a fast hold;
Balancing act of a trapeze,
    This is one's own office.

Up precipices, down the gut
Of cavernous earth
Armed with awkward tools
And a deep lust for gold
They kill or can be killed
    In this nasty sacrifice.

More often, dice falls badly
Gamble ending in death
Colleagues raising alarm
For rescue to be staged
To pull out injured or dead
    Fallen from the precipice.

Through the eyes of him who is averse to illegal mining of mineral resources.

23 Sept' 2013

Why You Crumple Fast

By the busy clinic gate I sat
  And, there an ugly sight I saw.
In they come and out they go
  Yet, they ever wilt like straw!

When I looked at myself
  I then cheered my own dope
That is found not on any shelf
  But inside me, called Hope!

*

Whether an incurable disease
I will always relent to cease.
For, Hope cures, Hope heals
I retain ounces disease steals.

The sharp axe of disease to hack
Why would you give your neck?
For more guts, pain to shrug
Do taste Hope the daring drug!

Dry Cleaner Next Door

Her mind is "dirt of the bush"
  In his hand, a wrist he held tight,
Took a whip and gave her a brush
  Till clean and sparkling bright!

Like a stormy summer weather,
  Punctuated with a human cry
I heard the sound of woman's leather
  Tanned to be soft and not dry!

Oblige thyself, filth to clean
  So that Love in the house will stand.
Man, find fault in being mean
  At giving out powers of thy hand!

If wives were like cotton rugs,
  You'd bring yours for a wash!
I'd scorch dead all the bugs
  By the power of my whiplash!

> *For how long then my dear God…*
> *She is mother to another poor sod!*

Teeth

Your fetid lips overflow
With a flaccid slur of fury
Love's teeth are wobbly!

The War of Minds

Why would you defeat
  Your enemy
With noise and energy,
When you can keep Camp
  Always intact
With tricks and tact?

Bottle disease
Silent murmurs of sorrow
In the bottle we sing
And, discover tomorrow,
Cash taken to the wing.

In the glass we confide
(Comforter worse than all)
Beer cannot bridle sorrow's tide
Although we howl in our call.

Wretched *Writher*

I am a *Writher* working hard
A trophy of glass to earn
Yet, each time mine is a shard
And, I continue to yearn.

Like a boxer, I throw a punch
To knock down my foe:
My plans always crunch
Or I step on my own toe.

I am a *Writher* that I know
A *Writher* of hidden fame
I will not, to pain kowtow
Till the day you read my name!

Liberty

Take away everything;
Take away my misery
Leave me with nothing;
You leave me with liberty.

Bereave me of wealth
Steal from me dearth
Gimme endearment
You've given me mirth.

For, a partner so inane
More so, impregnable
Is a wicked visitation;
A disaster so insufferable.

15 Jan' 2008, Chakari.

22

A Coward's Disease

Somebody should sell like a hot bun
Someone must be a subject for gossip:
Certain people suffer a rare malady;
They want to complain about nothing!

The spell becomes bad, or so I think
Especially when the man is a coward.
A coward's nerve is greatly invoked
Where the subject has shown his back.

He is aware he himself is pretty weak.
He therefore seeks honour through calumny.
He bruits abroad another's weakness
So as to remain the only one who's strong.

This is the noise afflicting a coward.
He has to preach much and travel far
Taking up arms in the field of gossip
To destroy someone else's good image.

This coward though rich has no peace
Not least perfection of his own image;
While chipping or chirping at others
Instead of attending to his own flaws!

Sun Down

At the cold dead of night
Before mother puts off the light
She sets the 'eating' table
To capture hunger the inner rebel.
Kango dishes done and sparkling clean
Inside closets they all lean.
She then locks up the door
Before falling on the floor.
Clothed in nightly attires
At last tired she then retires.

> Some people return to clay
> By the hard and harshest way:
> Just when he is still soft
> She falls from the Life's loft.
> While all children are still young
> He nods to the eerie tongue!
> While strong strolls his wife
> He loses his own merry life,
> Like scrambling for a train
> Leaving the granary empty of grain.
> For, wide agape is the Gate
> Consuming all born early or late!

> The Bell is aloud ringing;
> It's Sun Down we are going!

Rare Love, Rare Tree

Scholars opine and continue to argue
That the story is not quite true—
About a tree located "between"
Not being a tree verdant or green.

Still, others piety the sire Adam
And his devil-deflowered madam;
Whose lover who was unchaste
Brought him a curse in haste.

Sex was the real sinful scene
Only that the Book is not obscene!
The Book's miss of the bull's eye
Makes the whole story appear a lie!

Scenic Verses or Cynic Nerves

Thine is Epic Poetry.
Mine is relic Poetry:
  Debris of the poor's mirth
  After the storm of dearth.

Thine are sweet dreams.
Mine are sweat dreams:
  And plans, where others top
  Mine always flop!

Talks

Where's gone *ya'* tongue
Fallen down *ya'* throat
That *ya'* can't talk?

Frailty of Man Explored

Man has a right hand and left hand
A holy side and an evil side
A kind side and a cruel side
An inert side and inept side
Strong side and a weak side
A sad side and a happy side
     *

Most Human beings are right handed
Yet, they are extremely left-minded!
     *

Inert side overtakes the inept side
The Evil side surpasses the holy side
Happy side overpowers the sad side
Strong side supplants the weak side
Good side is clouded by the bad side
Not least, right side by the bad side
     *

Yet, Man endeavours to right the wrong
And not to wrong the *right* right!
Praying to be always right-handed
And, never at all, to be left-minded!

Justice

Have we grown up at all
Or we bubble like babies
Tantrums hitting Court Bells?!

Snakes of Industry

Forest of 'beacons' in the woods erupt
Marking territory called 'claims'
With silver 'plates' that look like grave plaques
Where lie some defunct diggers!

Long rods probe the dry ground,
As we trench the vast landscape.
We then cook soil called 'samples'
All in search of the shy yellowstone.

We sink deep and bottomless shafts
And cut tunnels through the rock,
Then seat steel piers into the holes
With dreary din here comes the Industry!

Eager man and metal together
Shake hands in unison of relay
With Conveyors handing over grit
To spinning drums named ball mills.

Cooking Pots: crucibles
At last spit out a yellow stone
Whose beauty can buy a man's soul
If he is reckless to peddle it!

The Amorphous Stone

Time heals a lot of wounds
As Time never stays put,
Rearing to pull its tired leg
Into an endless circle march.

Time also debunks myths,
Where movement of time,
Grinds into a minute pebble
An amorphous boulder.

As the hour hand tick 'talks',
Childhood fear wanes pale
And, blurred imagination
Assumes the shape of reality.

*First written in 1988, Chibwedziva Re-written, 31 Dec' 2012,
Chakari.*

Poem of Pain

He rolled both ashen eyes:
Injured, hamstrung, lame
Propped on side of his body.
Hissing, grimacing, writhing,
Incapacitated; quivering lips
Uttering unintelligibly
Amid the ungainly struggle—
In throe; in the agony
Of Prometheus in chains.
He could be thinking hard
Thinking of his children
As he gasped, determined
To stand up and to escape.
Alas! His back is crashed,
Legs dangle like gnarled sticks.
His hands are no use at all,
They've been severed clean…
Back of his head bursting
Covered in a cake of dirt.
Is there a creature left in this?
So frail and so vulnerable.

Moribund, macabre face's
Countenance, a cadaver's
"Alive enough to have strength to die!"*

Neutral Tones-Wessex Poems and Other Poems: Thomas Hardy.

Upon seeing a dying Chameleon run over by a passing car: and on "dreaming" of such pain as an epitome of Human suffering. Chakari, 3 Jan' 2013

Dread

A Dream come in the Day
Has cost him Darkness—
A crash-landed Angel!

Holy Cheater!

The Moon, the Sun and the Stars,
The Seas, Hills and the Mountains
Wind, Water and biting Frost
Heat, Cold and Warmness—

His Hand touched NOTHING
Then sprang ALL Forms of Life!

Grave Park Poesy

Spider webs…perhaps
Spiders stretch their own drapery
Beside his ashen shroud
And think they are handy
In burying a pauper!

Step by step, the strands weave
His gaunt legs
Picking string like a guitarist
Strumming songs of death
With shivering fingers.

Supine he lies, cold he lies
Hands beside his crispy flanks
Footfalls shuffling past
Living strangers in life's chores
Kicking dust like a mad bull!

What looks like a pillow
Is now a head stone
Not beneath his head as he lies
But above his forehead
Flat no more but upright

His name is engraved
His days of birth and death too.
He used to tint his scalp hiding age
Now the cold stone
Exposes his carnal folly!

Was his heart so black
For, what says the black stones
That mark his deathbed
When he was a flame
Whose apparel flowed so white?!

So, death ends all, it is true…
For, he sneezed to no end
When flowers drew nigh
Could it then be mischief
Of she who brought this bouquet?

He fought and conquered
He served when called.
They say he marched his men
Leaving no stone atop another
His is perpetually rooted.

Nor heed when we wailed
Who used to eavesdrop whispers,
Banter, gossip or grapevine.
Now, the din of wayfarers
Will not arouse his chalk self?

His neck swayed so well
To lady gaiety wriggling past
Would he gnaw death's string
And follow her wherever
Wherever she has strolled?

Better the dead hear no more
See no more, taste no more:
The nerd would spin in his casing
To hear his girl is pregnant
From a slovenly urchin!

The Wheel of Time

Life, just as time, is but an old wheel
Spinning and turning like a film reel.
See how life's wheel races
Overtaking the swift in their enduring paces
See also the film reel cast faces:
Sad faces, old faces, cold faces,
Happy faces, young faces
Pining for him donned on drapery laces
And thrust into holes dug deep
Wherein he embraces eternal sleep.
Hear how bereft faces with sorrow weep
For him now carefree time to keep…
So, their unshod and cracked heel
Merciless earth they stamp and race
While deaf slumbers the geek!

Park Of Bones

Oblivious to decomposing bones underneath
Hooked by bright wreath
Happy birds brooking of syrup
From stone to another hop and chirrup.

Would they know that 'other' colour bright
Is but sewn paper confusing sight
For, a lone woman heavy of womb
Left love's token on her dead husband's tomb!

Cenotaph

Great are they for whom this rock is chiselled and sandblasted!
(To they who perished let's all pay homage.)
But, what fate awaits them who butchered and or busted
Such a mass of men with wanton outrage?

Graves a mass; man and woman together buried—
Has the enemy taken stock of his brutal deed
When he blew sulphur in a manner so hurried
And left many innocent hearts to baulk or bleed?

Those who witnessed and by luck lived to tell
Relate how the youths and adults unarmed
Under bombardment so sudden defencelessly fell
With few survivors now permanently harmed.

Overcast with bombs the sky that day was clogged
Survivors of the horror relate with ire:
To the fleeing, muzzles, how futile they dodged
Mad choppers raining down relentless fire!

So, not on a platter was peace begot— far from it!
But through blood and tears and pain
And selflessness of they who lie embracing grit
Sacrifice of whom must not be in vain!

Conceived at Zaka near a small Heroes' Acre on 16 July 2018.

Powder Keg

I'm a rude punster please forgive the pun!
That I write of the keg is pure mischief.
For, I contemplate a body fried in a pan
To tar or ash and tied in a handkerchief,

By the shelf or by the torrent bestowed
And snuffed away by ancestors windward
Who enjoy the flavour of a home-ward
Coming progeny's genes in ashes stowed!

Rivers will silt, shelves may give in to weight
As more bodies fall in the fiery urn's bait.
Ancestors' nostrils too will jam like a keg
More powder being fed on a relentless leg!

Economics of saving space is exposed
When dead people are daily disposed.
Yet, the Book is a yardstick so straight
Guiding man on how to handle the fate:

In a grave hewn on rock Him they buried—
Whose surprise resurrection was so hurried—
For, *on the Third Day Christ rose to Life,*
His own pain and blood ending Man's strife!

A Baby Was He

A hole so small is all they show
Remains of baby he where they lie
He who saw not any tomorrow
When at two he said his goodbye.

Fifty years all have sped away
With him cold in the sodden clay.
(Wish he were a potato; underneath
That grow though choked of breath!)

Is he elder brother to his siblings
Who were all born after him?
Would they know him nor he them
Though a void voice lie in between!

He is a missing link or link so small
Along the jerking cord
For without him a chain is not tall
Feet of mirth the river to ford.

He lingers in his mother's air
In her sojourn of the cruel earth
That the first seed that did ill fare
Turned her a lasting farmer of dearth!

As I Am

As thus past they filed
Over me in the box supine
Was I chaffed or riled
By the moving line?

None observes so well
Man's soul and mind
Like he whose eye is shut
Where all perceive he is blind.

Did I properly hear or see
What, while down, I saw:
All one, two and three
Say: *Soon we'll follow*!

From men with sickly beard
Like a rolling stone
Sans moss, I also heard:
We are near— yours is done.

Women's legs were so clear.
So soft. No. Pulling socks
Pulled high as lustre could bear
I saw ALL dear folks!

With a left hand our offering
We deposit in lust's pit
We are a sick offspring
Soon, all headed into grit!

I'll Not Sing Now

This mouth that grit has stopped
Was Pavarotti's during my day.
A leg that is twisted; maybe chopped
Was Michael Jackson's at play.

You who're still healthy or still alive
Use your time well, be in mirth;
Like a sanguine bee in a beehive
Amassing nectar 'fore winter's dearth.

There is no thing as dying old or young
 It's about dying early or dying late:
Mind still fresh or then, so strong,
Overused or unused before fate!

The issue about ghosts— how true!
A dead soul who enjoyed less
For his lost time and out of rue
Stirs out of case in vengeance's dress!

Third Day

Roman Guards had taken post on the grave's Rock
To arrest Jesus should He, though dead, play His usual tricks!
Though hamstrung in a shroud, loud ticked His clock
That sundered rock; breaking to shard like earthen bricks!

The Third Day was a bad day to Roman snoozers
Who, presumably, paid the ultimate prize with their life,
The Roman Code of Conduct being austere to duty losers,
Could've been hanged as 'drowsy sons of a stupid wife!'

Why would the damn ladies continue to visit the dead
Is but a carnal wonder yet wrought from the Cloud
For their bargain, they witnessed a scene of pure dread:
A corpse presumed rotting had doffed and left his shroud!

Till Death Don't Us Part

A phenomena to culture unique and too strange
Almost nudged me my own will to alter or change.
A man infatuated with his wife, in the homestretch,
He warned her against marrying another wretch!

Too deep a grave he initiated its unique design
So that in one hole upon death the couple would align.
He thought if they shared a grave together, his heart
Would rest thus he called it: *Till Death Don't us Part*!

When his wife died first, he buried her too deep.
And left the upper deck empty for his future repose.
He waited a day or two and then stopped to weep.
Only culture knew: the fellow was ready to propose!

One day a lady approached him— so sweet a widow,
(Yet her heart with bereavement was being gnawed)
Introducing self with voice that cannot be ignored!

Her own woe she told: her man was also buried
Where he'd not escape though desperate he clawed:
He was also laid in a double-deck grave when he died.

She had mourned and mourned. The loss was deep.
A few days of weeping her 'appetite' was restored.
Society knows what's next when a widow stops to weep!

Love is soporific or a panacea if not a drug outright!
When flesh with wounds still fresh is pressed tight
The veins ripped apart and blood spilled so red
Heal instantly. In no time both conspired to wed!

Overjoyed with a new find, widow now sweet wife—
By the stealth of night alone he skulked— risking life—
Into the graveyard where his wife death embraced
To fill the upper deck which upon death he'd have graced.

That preposterous day the world overturned with rage
Reality tussling lies in their usual world wrestling cage.

The two never again played Angel with a carnal mind!

Yellow Like Cheese

So was the musician King Yellow
Whose voice was sweet and mellow.
With mirth he sang his soul and heart
Sang it sweet through Reggae's art!

He was an Artist so marvelled
For the tint unique and unparalleled
Yet, his lyrics left an indelible spoor
Printed in Jamaica's dance floor!

The higher the mountain
The cooler the breeze
The younger the lady
The tighter the squeeze!

An enchanted singer moving hearts
With bravura that topped the charts
Said he: *Yellow Man is the only one…!*
Who'd else would resist the tone?

*

Prejudice is a ravenous louse
That quaff concealed in a blouse—
King Yellow suffered a rare drama:
He was rejected by his own Ma!

Who, of all living people, is like him
For suffering a woman's whim?
Who for the paleness of his skin
She thrust the infant in a street bin?

47

Zungunzungunguzunguzeng....
Creative his voice and unique the slang;
Yellow Man's the only One!
That's how his sorrow in art was done!

*

Don't look at yourself with rue
Nor regret your skin's tint or hue.
You might be a star-in-waiting
Tomorrow's model in your travailing.

We're goin' London summer Holiday
So on and so forth did he play.
Would you like to go with me?
Would you like to go Rosie...?

All you who are still alive this heed:
Mankind must toil for his own feed!
Rise above your carnal infirmity
You'll enjoy success to infinity!

Funny Fare!

(Letter from the Dead!)

Don't vote for him, please vote for me
Vote for change and things so new
I'm a road straight to your destiny
A cloth to those who cry— real and true.

With no cement I'll build where others failed
Though with no rivers I'll build bridges
All murderers will be bailed from jail
For Eskimos, I pledge reliable fridges!

Investors will come like a flood
To mine all over and employ the infirm
The country will be awash with food
Ask Minister of Propaganda to confirm!

I'll talk to God to Heaven all be booked
Who wishes to go today I'll chart a flight
Pack you all, the upright and the crooked
Then elude the wicked world's plight!

Our Courts will henceforth be corrupt
Such that it'll be difficult to go to jail
Who'll the drunkard divorcing interrupt?
You'll rule yourselves and I'll only trail!

Virgins buried with Shaka's mother
Priority of my tenure will be to exhume
And bestow them a properly famished brother,
An appropriate task to reproduce resume!

Who'll be equal on the scales of justice
(To weigh what when equal be all things?)
Thief by way of brevity had a lot to sacrifice
I'll take the nerd off culpability's strings!

Hospitals will all be open and so ready
The healthy to admit in order to taste
Medicine and see what makes him steady
Then claim it with unbridled haste!

Our schools too, will all the loafers enrol
Laze around in colleges with a stipend
Though failed, enter Government payroll
And the fiscus burden to near no end!

All Churches will burn to free the nun
Trapped in garments of over-size drapes
And, ordained brother, while holding a gun
Will baptise with malt or sour grapes!

Ha, ha, ha! Vote for the one and only one
Who'll feed all of you when you're asleep
Who'll tune your snores to a mellow tone
And like Angels sighing all those who weep!

Come in your dozens my pretty goons
You know no-one lying better than me
Come eat moon's cheese with your very spoons
I'll show you voters, how I'll stupefy thee!

*

Man's mind is not level all the time
Whenever hungry; his brain is sick.
Introduce a favour, like a good clime,
It thaws his chill like a frozen chick!

On that leg; is there anything so fair,
Free or credible in such a process
Where choice is influenced by flair—
Voter's inclination by 'sweet' duress?

When corruption sinks to the bone
For a smile he wears a snarl and sneer.
And growl with an eerie or devilish tone
When he means to sing with cheer!

Such men live with a Freudian slip
Yet, at contrition alter, die with a baulk—
For, the inner man suffers a double dip
Till he tears cover yearning to talk!

All the puke and pout is never true
Their desire is to make you a fool.
Plea though eloquent is pee and poo
To enable them to rule and rule!

Take them not so serious my folks
They're a hawker trading man's heart
(Or, as a hooker to the wind who talks!)
Not all attune to their field of art!

*

To such when alive once I fell prey
My tired mind pinned to that then this

51

Till one day gives in to another day
Never my heart at once tasted bliss.

Complain to the President you chose
Look how he refers to the Minister
Then the Minister his door he closes
Spurning your dialectics called sinister!

Did you elect the Minister my folks?
The President campaigned aloud
Were you not hooked by his very talks
Who now is acting reverse or proud?

Remove the title of President please
Are people not tired with his roles nil?
Prefer instead Senior Minister to ease
Crisis of title so sick it needs a pill!

Senior Minister will not rule as King
But supervisor of Ministers to mark
Their home work; and not just blink!
Then correct their error with a spark!

Long Time

What would words mean to him
The ancient and the long dead
Vocabulary being not for his whim
But for ours to crack our head?

What would the racy Zebra Cross
Mean to the old hunter's syntax
Perhaps a point a missile to toss
And game kill with recoil of an axe!

Crossing place leading to school
With a big girl holding a little boy…
Maybe a sweet decree or a rule
Youngster to marry and to enjoy?

When you in the game area drive
A signpost with a leaping kudu see
Shaka would muse— had he been alive—
Of a hunting licence with no fee!

A car on a slop that seems to drop
Would send the ancients to scurry
For fear of machines on their top
Falling and crashing them to puree!

Today as cars you see carrying loads
The old to board could've refused!
Such is my story concerning roads
And the old who along rarely used!

Wise Poor

Gimme not a horde too huge
If plenty makes the mind dull.
Bestow just enough for a refuge
I only need a head with knowledge full.

While they anguish for richness
And its quest diligently stage
Will they not languish in dullness
To rue later purity of the sage?

I need no Heaven nor the Earth
If my mind by half will wilt
But, gimme want, gimme dearth
Wisdom mixed in mirth with it!

Dead Semantics

I died a non-teacher but an icy dumb.
In this desolate box, a cold case in which I lie
Will I rue my day with the rule of thumb,
Or, post word to those who one day will die?

In episode way, the grey and green I'll teach
Perchance they'll one day a hazard eschew:
Kids run first in the road the other end to reach
With no traffic movement's fatal clue!

No less, the overindulgent, who run hands
In the pocket trapped in frenzy of the spree
Who next day hesitate in same pockets to run hands
Afraid to know amount left of the spree!

*

A good *lesson* to learn
And, a reward to earn
Is: look 'fore you leap
Or, look 'fore you weep!

An *irony* from the story
Deduce with fair glory:
All climbers with haste
Soon, they lie to waste.

An *allegory* of this clip
I'll tell with my dead lip:
Diverse may be a name
Men an' kids think the same!

*

Refrain man of clod, reframe from lure of the looks
Most beautiful things have in their inside hidden hooks.

The sweetest thing that when you eat or taste with lip
Titillates has in it bane dropping clear like holy oils drip;

Talk to rich men and hear their affliction or bitter pain:
Tarty food in their tummy soaks the heart with pure bane!

They toddle as they walk, they who must be so strong
While a lank fellow, with visible vitality, springs along!

*

Who said don't eat your wealth
Or you'll walk with stealth?!
Who says to beauty disdain
Or, from sweets, do refrain?

Moderation is name of the game
Over-indulge; eat to near bloat
We'll give you another name
For bleating as a tethered goat!
I'm dead and was buried deep
My perspective is now wide
See the skull's eye socket deep
I now can see across the divide!

Those who call it 'death's grin'
Have semantics pretty pure.

Who, like Me, so flexed his chin,
Shouting it all so sure?

Bones

I saw a country with no town
Every creature lived in glee
From worm in the soil down
To a bird up the green tree!

When engines turned over bones
And sprouted the brick wall
Birds of air cut cheery tones
Until the rain stopped to fall!

When nature is tightly sealed
Man's mind by sin is swayed:
When Adam a crotch concealed
God read his heart had strayed!

When soil is rived by a plough
It over-turns the reposed dead
He who dies has had enough
Let him be and rest his head!

Bonds

As here I lay and them there
I heard one of them cry:
Why did they inter me here
I'm not a hero it's a lie!

At the same time then I saw
On the cenotaph a witch
Digging deep with her claw
For a corpse in the ditch.

Dawn, I heard in the gloom:
Much effort have I wasted
The grave 'thing' is not a tomb
But a slab! She detested!

Then the awful nakedness
And the disappointment—
She stole away nonetheless
In her *embonpoint!*

To the complaining dead
Who his being no hero
Was source of his aching head
There my eye I did throw:

Look, I was almost licked
By the witch hero-hunting
Thank God a cenotaph she picked!
Damn. He was punting!

What heroes have we got
And which witches do we have?
Who chooses who or not
And where their grave to pave?

The tight bond of witches
And their erstwhile heroes
Is marked by empty ditches
And liars' own throes!

Golgotha

To each his own cross
Jesus carried His.
To each his sword
No more baby bliss.
For, another will die
Golgotha is nigh.

Look at the bones
Moving in a bag...
The bag; a kin
Like a helpless stag
He soon will be rust
A sword when thrust.

Run not those legs
So weary with strife
Parry not the blow
That took Son's life—
Those in power will
Ever have power to kill!

Hungry crows await
Bone of he in pangs
Knowing too well
Soon 'nother surely hangs
For, the lip will stop
Not to say: STOP!

Alone

I, back to life, sprang forth almost
The Grave Park scene of candour
Stirring with fashion white as frost
Dead hearts pulsated with its splendour.

Ladies, for they are women no more,
In dark glasses minding their poise
More than what the day had in store!
For the said grief, I heard no noise!

There was opulence in the car park
(And in their wardrobes, *hot couture.*)
Man and, what? Ladies, dining till dark
Celebrating my passage to the future.

When I looked with a smarting eye
For, that's an only glimpse God allowed,
I saw my dishevelled wife pitiably cry
Invariably so, my son who followed.

The crowd waned, leaving me to my end
A bevy of cars too, melting away.
And I was alone in the invisible hand
In my cold case like a stowaway!

Nature's Embrace

When at last I die
Put not pillars of gold
Wherein cold I lie
But Sheena's Gold.

No even silver case
Will my heart enchant
But Zinnia in a vase
The rest to plant!

Let Gardenia bloom
Where Three Sisters
Torch away gloom
With petal flickers,

Around the Park
Bougainvillea border
The yard in dark
With crimson order!

Rosellia Whippy whip
Do deeply desire
Mischievous to strip
And spank with ire!

Caladium's tinted leaf
Turns a dead heart
To, from his own grief,
Attune to nature's art!

Let Strawbelanthus be
In its purple colour
Flap beauty to me
And end death's dolour.

With Cordline so red
And Dracaena large
Let eye sockets be fed
I'll pay the charge!

Hard Work Not Gifted

Count me not as he gifted
But as one who worked so hard
What happens: if well-gifted
Then elude to sweat it hard??

If so hard I work poor me
Not gifted being well too aware
Will I not bring to thee
The lazy gifted will not dare!?

Talk not of innate talent
Unattended it will crush.
Inborn ability is too latent
In this world ruled by rush!

*

By the bright candle light
I sweat it out without a break
Days turn into the night
A yoke of Letters by my neck!

Who'll lighten the heavy boulder
Pulled by me a poor cow?
For, square on my shoulder
Pain of effort is all I know!

*

This talk I dared deliver
For, man lives just only once
Regard yourself a toil believer
And regain the lost chance!

I Wish For No Other World

The world four Cardinal Points has it.
Me too when my hands are stretched:
Look closely as cold I lie in the pit:
Head and feet plus hands outstretched!

Didn't I, elusive world, at last regain,
Sorrow squashed, alive anew am I;
Who once was dead with carnal pain
'Fore in my lone post peacefully lie?

*

Let's discuss it with words so frank
(Wish it's not a hornet's nest that I prod!)
Lie not down with rue on your flank
Nor to death, with a pending duty, nod;

That's "lying self down with a whip!"
(Sounds true of dead him with no will.)
For, he the gods should in the bud nip
Must be he who leaves a settled bill!

*

While the summer sun shines bright
Soil, damp and fertile, with humus
Harvest not your hay with delight
Instead, plant more to harvest a mass!

As time closes-time for you to leave—
Who uncovered regrettably will remain
To mourn, to travail and to grieve
In loss of dross plus bereavement's pain?

Put-In

God created man to live and be strong
Never did He create a sloth to eat
God will find in the weaklings as wrong
For eluding labour to live by cheat!

In a body fit or strong you'll also find,
Saddled and sitting hard and steady,
Not malleable a brain but strong a mind
To pain of hardship that's ever ready.

*

Put-In's vitality in the Siberian breezes
And in the submarine that freezes...
If God snapped open my box of decay
Would I not relive life the Put-In way!

Put-In, the real epitome of will power,
Will he to any man kowtow or cower?
Even when down, spirit of never-say-die
His wings unfurls to once more fly high!

*

The world awaits their brawns and brevity
The strong and the spirited in mind
To lift up all suffering Humankind
From poverty's crashing load and gravity.

Let man's brawns built bridges not hedges
Prejudice, from his inner heart evacuate

Instead, in eyes of the law all man equate
The poor and the powerful men of all ages!

*

Let not the strong contemplate in a spirit of defeat
When, for purposes of a treaty, they retreat.

Strength is not tested in times of gratitude
But during moments of helpless solitude.

Strength, power, nay fortitude is a treasure
If, when weighed, it moves up the measure.

Where 'it' bends a man down his foe to inter
Then, he no longer has any power to declare!

If the weak who finds another as he bled
Nurses him home though on a cranky bed;

His forte is known. His brawns have whacked
To what self-guilt Macho would've quaked!!

*

Regan and Gobachev when set on the table
Perestroika marked their bubble as affable.
Them who looked at another with a glance:
In Putin and Obama we lost a chance.

Look not to Africans, the Nations strong,
As if to medieval times they belong
Nor regard human resource mentally poor
Land, for resources a shopping floor!

Real men wielding power and influence
Flex brawns of the heart and of brain
To explore weak man's repressed intelligence
And his perceptible flaw disdain!

If I were to live again since I'm now dead
I'd rise in Obama's gaiety of head!
No less adeptness and agility of his frame;
Wisdom and wit marks my 'dog's' name!

A Giant's Shoes

I've waited for dead man's shoes
Wondering if it'll fit from heel to toes
When at last the Giant man passed
I was, by the size, quite nonplussed!!

I held high the boots and aloud said
"Will these small toes fit I'm afraid?"
Yet, a voice nearby clearly did I hear:
"They're your Dad's, you must wear!"

Really? My Dad was a giant in heart
Yet, his tongue, not a hill but a wart!

After years of fleeting back I came
And found the boots still the same.
Someone asked why I was so evasive
I shouted: "They're too expensive!

"I'm he who came after, it's not a lie
"Yet not fit his shoe strings to untie!
"Pray I be pure, for I'm still too base."

Moon Eclipse

What does it mean when the moon is obscured?
Some suggest it has all decayed
To Divinity others turn and are 'told' what occurred:
"Second Coming is not at all delayed."

Others opine still: "Michael and the Devil are in a fight,
"As they tussle, their shadow
"Obscures the Moon or the Sun's radiant light."
Yet, the Devil's naked and narrow!

No man watches the eclipse as good as the dead
Thus, a better answer do desire
Supine as they lie waiting with a propped forehead
For a day they'll once again suspire!

27 July 2018, Chiredzi.

Gravy Powder

1
It so happened one day when there lonely I lay
For Deadman was I and one quite rested too
As shadows three, wish they were shadows real,
 In full nakedness into the park graveyard they came.

Of the three the dreadful 'things' two were males
And, the ugliest of all threesome; a one woman.
From grave to grave, all naked they skulked.
With baited feelings her legs at most I saw.

I'm dead. No? But women, clearly I recall
Although I now lie alone with no suitor at all.
Women, in all their nakedness, don't I know?
Know especially for the layout of their legs?!

Kill me if you will, but what have you to kill,
Am already dead! For, guys, the lady's legs….
From knee up to you know where, soft bumps
Turned her thighs to a sack of potatoes!

Then I said to myself: Isn't the bumpy-thigh lady shy,
Both her brazen companions being full males;
While two males in uniform nudity themselves—
Wonder of wonders— not equally ashamed?

One of the males I saw, or so I thought,
(Sometimes I wonder why I think certain things)
Appeared quite dutiful and so active although
He had for a foot a perfect hockey club!

So gaunt appeared the fellow, if my dead eyes
Or, if my dead brain is anything to go by.
The guy's countenance was actually punctuated
By a forest for hair and thicket for a beard.

The same spooky guy, or so it seemed, was
More caring to the woman whom I so suspected
Though being a witch, she was also his bitch
With caution as he chaperoned her around graves.

But, the third Apparition, what a gentleman!
He must've been well educated of all the wizards!
For, his core interest was to diligently read
Inscriptions engraved on the forest of headstones.

Then, with a marked wry of a irked connoisseur
Adeptly as he did so, closely schemed round
And round the Park checking and eliminating
 Several graves for whatever he seemed to detest;

While cutting a funny physique with bend legs
Rickets of which exuded the impression
And posture, if not an appearance of a giant dog
Too busy doing the elimination business!

2
There in my cold self as I lay, too nonplussed
As to the daring Apparitions' mission of terror,
Busy as usual, as graves the threesome scanned
To desolate mine at last the Shadows stopped.

Stooped, the educated one squinting, then uttered:
No head stone with data but a concrete cross.
He threw his hands up bored: *I wonder if there's
Any meaningful corpse lying down this slab*!

73

At that dreadful instance the lady was astride
The tomb stone where dead I supine I so lay.
Said she: *How then do we know he was not a child*
When he died or a fully grown up chap?

Guys! In my own dead self a close up I snatched;
 The Witch's chubby potato bag legs hit my face
As deliciously she strode above my bones wishing
I had anymore piece of 'flesh' to my name left,

To father more ghost children with the witch
For, so plumb and so appetising was she.
As I roiled in my own dead man's desire however
Aloud squeaked the gaunt Club Foot Ghost:

Man or child inside who cares good fellows!
Pointing the cross: *He must've been a Christian*
Or so I suppose. Due to assertive morals,
Though he be big, for a meal he is too lean!

3
Well presumed, with one leap, sailed club foot
Across my grave and landed elsewhere next.
But, as he hit the ground, his foot he scanned
With measured carefulness and dire concern.

Perhaps, or so I thought, the curved 'thing'
Could sometimes give the gaunt Ghost a difficult,
Yet the velocity of his giant leap carried with it
Agility, frenzy, fury and ferocious execution.

Had it been a game of hockey, surmised dead I,
Couldn't he have slapped and threw a perfect score?

Alas! In his restive nature, such stamina was
However, wasted on mere nocturnal grave shopping!

As thus I mused, it was the educated whiz
 Who my fixated 'eyes' from the club man drew
And from feelings of the witch's embonpoint
Toward more details of his unique industry!

There near where I lay, on a large tombstone
Almost like a pedestal, beckoned he to the other
Remarking: *Dig it open, shall we. He must be*
A big bloke who down here lies. He reads the plaque*:*

IN HONOUR OF HE WHO FELL, WHO WIDOWS
DEFENDED WITH HIS BIG HEART
AND THE POOR PROTECTED WITH STRONG ARMS,
THE BARREN WITH HIS OWN MANHOOD!

The three with frenzy fell onto the desired spot
As creatures rapacious vying for an elusive meal!
Like blind moles of blind minds, they barrowed
And scooped soil till a mount grew high as a hill!

As dawn stole in with its stroke of russet rays
In a huff, one, two and three out emerged, they,
Soiled like sweet potatoes just dug out of the soil.
Time which the educated fellow aloud freaked:

It's not a tomb, my mistake, it's a damn cenotaph.
Hurry up let's away go for dawn is stealing in
And we haven't made good out of our day yet. Said he.
At that, Club Foot, headed for a large tombstone
Exclaiming: *Look guys, it's almost like a house,*
How big! Certainly our effort will at last be paid

75

And home we'll go ribs pulsating with real feed
Wouldn't the 'night of long teeth' have been accomplished!

4

I craned a brittle neck to see the said structure.
They are those graves or as monuments expensive
Only the opulent often in them repine. When 'he' was
Interred I was here already, hey! What fanfare!

From the choicest grey rock the structure was cut
A type so rare; at least, in this whole world.
The Head Stone too; so rich and well-engraved.
Invariably, Flowers regularly laid there atop.

The man's widow so often I see her here come.
Sometimes, on tow, the man's daughters two.
Ah! Nowadays they're quite grown-ups I guess,
From when he was here by a hearse deposited;

The procession; how traffic in town it froze…!
The din, the long dead corpses in this quarter
All almost stirred awoke! The City Father too
The funeral he attended and pitiably mourned!

Then nodded I as thus I thought the educated
Witch had, also for his meticulous choice, wit.
The finger of the egghead being indisputable;
The indefatigable three with spirited resolve assailed!

The tomb slab they upset. The dutiful Club Foot
With one wild last chance leap descended
The dead man's bedroom of pain and sadness
Whiz kid or wizard bucking his awkward orders!

Yet could I've heard the man's vexations

Inside the gloomy depth the wretch descended
Nor, would I've properly seen his confusion
Till when with a small tin parcel he emerged?

And the rest of the greedy and expectant company.....
Damn. Shouted the Learned Ghost. *This isn't*
A corpse, it's a tin. We aren't machines' gear boxes
What use is metal for a meal, we need real flesh?

Then, pointing a finger: *Open it*. With a thin neck
The chubby woman peeped then with mirth cried:
Hurray, powder! Ah guys! This is gravy powder!
But the fastidious Learned Instructor was distraught.

Drew he near, smelled the tin, then exclaimed:
The fellow must've been an armed Gangster,
What an ending, he died and lay with his gun powder!
But, differed Club Foot: *No. It's snuff! Where's the sniffer?*

As thus they argued, all on my grave they squatted
Quite oblivious to the impending day break-
Endlessly as they argued on how best the finding
Could be utilised having been obtained by accident.

But all seemed a consensus to reach, as the find,
Supposedly seemed serendipity. But the hurdle:
Who'd claim it on another's behalf being witches
Living each alone, lacking in trust of each other?

5
Look, I'm a woman. Am good at broth-making.
The Potato Legs said. *So, I'll take it, mix it*
With human milk, it'll then be a perfect pudding.
We'll then meet somewhere to enjoy powdered flesh!

The boon of powder gravy, tart or pudding is that
In a single gulp, guys, you've eaten a whole damn corpse
From scalp to toe. Said she moving to claim the tin.

No, no, no! Exclaimed the argumentative Club Foot.
This is pure and mature snuff. Let's share it and
With just one sniff you would've staffed in the nose
The whole dead celebrity and his hoarded wealth!

No guys. Learned Ghost with calculated fluency said.
I think, he clears his throat, the needless pause
Of which was to draw his company's attention:
Gun powder is handy at shooting dead survivors!

With airs, again he clears his patched throat;
Then, the dead and the fresh ones we'll bag
From our own hunting and not from parlours alone.
He seems to grab the tin while the two refuse.

6
But, sometimes I presuppose my eyes are sharp.
So sharp, especially when it is night time. Although
It was then daybreak. So, from the woods I espied
A furtive face following up witches' *impasse.*

The furtive wretch seemed to have a better idea.
To his own idiosyncrasy, he was a Grave Robber!
So, the effort of his industry would've paid off
If successfully he snatched away the disputed tin!

Thus on his belly he crawled, as there and then
The nocturnal trio argued with endless posturing.
As a fish eagle, in one fell swoop, the tin was gone;
Clung tight inside the strong arm as he tore off.

Helter-skelter poured the threesome behind
Giving a wild chase. The woman in her nakedness
Lamenting: *My gravy tin*! And, the agile Club Foot:
My snuff! Not outwitted, the whiz: *My gun powder*!

Through the industrious street the party gave chase
While the lucky trump, ahead of all the naked lot,
Discordantly shouting: *Holy Snuff, Gun Powder!*
The naked Dame freaking mad: *Gravy Powder Soup*!

7
It must've been quite a spectacle, a human being,
Inside his arm, clutching a bright tin and running
At breakneck speed, behind, three naked 'things':
Club foot, rickets and chubby thighs giving chase!

What at daybreak, middle of town happened,
My folks, who knows? Here in my death, not I.
But one thing for sure: witches, the thief and tin
All left the dirty grave yard at alarming speed!

At last, tiredness, by my neck tie it grabbed
Shoving poor I into a crispy and ethereal whiff
Carrying man with its wings to the serene world
Where souls; living or dead, with amity unite!

Man O' Clay

i

There's a stick at end of a lollipop
Thus, abruptly sweetness is known to end.
Man, invariably, is just a clay dollop
When dry which breaks when bend!

Am a jealous God, that I need not remind…
Who else among man immortal
And had in it more of a genius mind
To create a man like me so eternal?

Clever boys don't cry remember!
Wipe the tears dry and take your post
Know well at end of January is a December
End of summer heat, winter frost.

If matter was immortal, just think,
Where would vegetables get manure?
Ground, as rock… where would you sink
A peg to mark the way to the future?

If babies remained babies as you formulate
From where would father I secure
The spacious world with bliss to populate
As pain of loss seems not to find a cure?

If forever an old remains so old
Incapacitated even a child to father
Yet hesitant to approach his eternal fold
Earth so scarce; man would live on top of another!

Who then do you want to punish
For each one of man a world to create
And, do it with speed of man's wish
Meeting each second children to procreate?

ii

Man out of clod and spat sprang forth
Then a woman from a man's rib
Now you want me to be your mother
Whose clod is in the womb bearing twins

When the old dry clod breaks with age
You want me to spit and remould it
To spring forth crouching twins
That want to marry just as they are born?

Am I a foolish God; Baal would you say
Who breaks into shard when felled
Yet claims potency even to raise man
When he himself cannot even stand up?

Would you test your God and live
When both legs in a torrent you put
The depth to fathom-that is if you're luck
Away not to be swept and drown in sin!

Am I the one taking dead people as you say
Or, when a person dies as thus you cry?
Look, I made man and put him on earth
It's his choice to come to me dead or alive!

Yet, when he dies, am I surprised at all
What may surprise perhaps is the manner of his dying

For, some die young and innocent
While others die while murdering another!

Death. Is death unique when life is not?
Who wants to live forever- you tell me
Or, perhaps forever remain young
For both kind of men are not living at all?

Grow up, marry, you got another mother
The way she patched up bruises
Wife-mother has no reason to relent
What a better mother with roles doubled!

But soon, she is someone else's very mother
Before he ferrets the neighbourhood
For a night nurse bruises to patch
With her hot and prehensile tongue!

Daughters too, they look for fathers
By inspecting loin cloths with erect fingers
And when they find their elusive father
They bear some more callous bastards

Who denies to die and say God's not fair
When fairness is subject to ambiguity of semen
And semantics and Eve's amour
Who raped Adam while the Snake witnessed
Head poised to bite if he fled the session!

Those who refuse to die
Refuse with clenched teeth to Regain Lost Paradise
For the seed of sin must die
As purgatory before Judgment Day!

Age is the penalty for sin good as death
So, STOP crying and pray for penance
Perchance your sins will cease
And, you shall in Heaven die no more!

iii

A good cue from Jesus you better take
For, He died and Third Day up He rose
If your heart this Faith does partake
Then no more will your mind be morose!

For, as the old sun at last dies at dusk
Dawn will *chase away *gloom with a bowl of light*
As Omar Khayyam's poetic musk
Romantically celebrated the end of night!

For, when in each grave Angels of life
With radiance torch or touch
Tombs will crack breaking the bond of strife
Old, infirm or full to life will spring and not crouch!

Then, you'll know I'm God your God
Who created man and in him breathed life
And, know thyself as clod that manufactured sin
And breathed in it death and strife!

*The Rubaiyat of Omar Khayyam: translated by Edward FitzGerald.

Hold it, Be Calm

Unless the seed for years stored
Where no moth has access to mottle
The most precious and most adored
Of its kind must leave the comfy bottle;

And in sodden earth so helpless fall
With dirty hands sealed and ignored
Will verdure spring forth from fall
And display nature's beauty long ago stored?

Dirt and mud and moisture mixed
Will the good seed mercilessly cover
Until the day that God has fixed
Out of all the rot beauty He'll uncover!

First he dies. Then on his tomb a wreath.
At the Last Call, finally defeats his fate!
For, unless a man succumbs to death
How'll he reach the Heaven's gate?

No Man as He

Had he been Adam, wouldn't he have the Snake reviled?
If Pharaoh, would he need an omen Israel to set free?
But as Michael and Abednego by Deities not defiled
And, as Daniel, life he sacrificed with no fear and for no fee!

From Here when at eKapa I look, there I see a mount
Whose rise I presume is caused by a big heart!
It's he now reposed, whose cost no man can count
Yet, whose visage is borne in each heart and every chart;

It's he the son of God: Nelson Rolihlahla Mandela!

Written 18 July 2018 in Chiredzi. Remembering Nelson Mandela.

About the author

Matose was born in a Shangane family on 27 October 1968 as Josefa Chauke. His father was a Reverend of the Free Methodist Church of the United States of America. His mother suffered from schizophrenia, forcing his father to marry a second wife.

After years herding cattle as a boy, Matose went to school in 1978 aged 10 at Gozonya in Hippo Valley Estates. It is at this time that upon obtaining a birth certificate, he was renamed Joseph Matose, which enabled him to enrol for Grade 1. His date of birth was also reduced to 26 November 1970 to enable him to be accepted as within the acceptable age.

This arrangement further facilitated payment of school fees directly from his guardian's wages who was a labourer in the Estate. His name was Salane Mathosi.

He later went to Chibwedziva Secondary School south of Chiredzi Town near the border with Mozambique between 1994 and 1987, learning beneath trees and roofless classrooms. It is at this school that Joseph met with University students employed as teachers during their semester holidays, who nurtured his interest in reading and writing.

Mentored by University of Zimbabwe scholars, Matose managed to discover his creative mind, thereby winning many rewards in composition-writing competitions at the school and adjacent schools.

In order to further nurture his creativity, Matose was introduced to the works of author Dambudzo Marechera and other Africa writers such as Ngũgĩ wa Thiong'o, Chinua Achebe, Okot p'Bitek, Charles Mungoshi and many more. However, Dambudzo remains his inspiration to this day.

While enjoying the lime-light of creativity and winning awards and the invaluable tutelage from University of Zimbabwe Scholars one of whom stood out prominent as Nkosana Hleruka, Matose was expelled from school for what was said to be "violent behaviour, beer-drinking and resistance to school authorities."

Fortunately, a cousin-brother schooled at Idaho University in the States of America, recently come home with a Bachelor's degree in Literature and a Master's degree in Divinity, now Principal of a newly opened Boarding School near the border with South Africa, called Malipati High, heard of Joseph's fate and reasons thereof. He quickly arranged that "the wretch" be delivered to his custody for better control and utility of "his writing skills."

1990. Matose was then housed in a room turned into a library, affording him the opportunity to read throughout the night. From here he continued writing poetry and prose to the delight of his cousin-brother who enlisted his skill to help translate a novel entitled: 'The Mourned One' into Shangane. However, the project did not come to fruition as the cousin brother passed on a few years later, after parting ways. Matose had suddenly left for South Africa in search of employment.

While working on the Farms, especially ZZ2 group of Farms in the Low Veld of South Africa, Matose continued to write poetry whose leitmotif was love, nostalgia, pain and suffering. At one point, he was employed as a cleaner at a Library in Petersburg where a chance meeting with University Students rekindled his love for reading and composing. Many a time he wrote poems and sold to students to earn a pittance as he tramped at a sleazy Railway Station with nowhere to go.

Yet, in between the sporadic forays into South Africa, Matose in 1995, managed to visit Rusape where Dambudzo Marechera grew up. He chanced upon the surviving young brother Nhamo Marechera, a veteran of the Liberation Struggle who was an heir to the cache of classic books left by Dambudzo. This was pure serendipity. Matose read and read. Chaucer, Wordsworth, Coleridge, Alan Poe, Virgil, Milton, Alighieri, Khayyam, Propertius. Poets and Philosophers of renown. Many more books were bestowed to Matose by Nhamo as a gesture of friendship. Until today the gifts are safely kept as invaluable possessions.

This interaction with Nhamo ended after a period of twelve months when he, like his brother Dambudzo, passed on from what looked like an excessive indulgence in alcohol while staying at Mandeya Township, on the banks of Rusape Dam, less than 5km from the rural home where the Marecheras lived. This untimely death disrupted the pending collaboration in a book entitled 'The Diary of Holidays'. The project fizzled out, robbing Matose of poems he had left in his partner's custody awaiting compilation into a manuscript.

The remaining Rusape renditions will be collected into a book entitled: Rusapwe!

Having had a young wife and a baby at a tender age of 23, Matose decided to settle down averse to searching for elusive employment opportunities in South Africa. He then joined a Security Company as a Security Guard in 1996.

Gifted in the art of writing, he worked his way up the ladder, becoming a Security Manager in a short space of time.

Matose who lives in Kadoma with wife Portia and five Children, one of whom is an international Watercolour Artist, is still employed as a Manager, Farmer, Writer and a struggling entrepreneur.

He writes poetry, short stories and novellas in the English Language.

Lightning Source UK Ltd.
Milton Keynes UK
UKHW040627281022
411251UK00001B/84

9 781914 287237